In Praise of Essex

In Praise of Essex

Edited by Frederic Vanson

Debbie Wing
Bodhewog
Llandissilio

EGON PUBLISHERS LTD
Meeting House Lane, Church Street, Baldock, Herts

First published in 1980
by Egon Publishers Ltd
Meeting House Lane, Church Street
Baldock, Herts

Bookjacket photography by Dennis Mansell

Typeset and printed by
S. G. Street & Co Ltd
Meeting House Lane, Church Street
Baldock, Herts

EDITOR'S NOTE

I was born in Metropolitan Essex but from an early age I have loved all of our county. Editing this anthology of contemporary poetry on Essex has been therefore a labour of love.

Essex seems at this time to be particularly rich in poetic talent, as indeed it has always been. I believe some of the poetry included here to be of the highest order and the average level of achievement to be a high one.

I should like to have included more poems in the traditional forms but one has to select from what has been written. Certainly there is no obscure pseudo-clever verse here but a selection of poetry which is intelligible, sincere and skilled.

It will be seen that many of the poems reprinted here first appeared in Essex Countryside *whose enlightened editor, Mr Eric Scott, deserves the thanks of all poetry lovers in the county.*

The poets here included are worthy successors of a great Essex, and English tradition. I hope Essex will take a proper pride in them.

F.V.
Harlow, 1980.

Copyright © Egon Publishers Ltd
ISBN 0 905858 14 X

CONTENTS

COUNTRY MATTERS

SEA, RIVER AND ESTUARY

Persons

And All That

(Harold Godwinson, king of England, died 1066. Buried at Waltham Abbey behind high altar)

You lie stiff in your paperback fame
one of history's props, your date and name
a fulcrum for the schoolboy pedant.

But lean to with that kingly sleight of hand,
battle-weary intent by a lake of burning sand.
Your fragile crown marked down 'ex-royal',

Your target eye a magpie in this game of kings
(Confessor's ghost has mind to higher things!).
How soon does Death make History of us all.

Poor King Cadaver, borne to a bullfrog's groan,
Essex bound to rest his yearling throne
amidst the Saxon twilight of the heaving oaks.

Whiplashed by monkish prayers that crack the air
(details of religion and realm now William's prayer).
Set down on Waltham's soil this gingerbread king,

devoured to a crumb in ambition's dog-teeth
and garland freedom for England's wreath . . .
then awake, sire, in your millenium —

with Harold still a remembered name
amidst proposed piazzas and games
of development we tilt and void

like escalated shopping for footsore wives
and cavernous parks where motorists dive.

STANLEY J. THOMAS

from CANTOS FOR ALFRED TENNYSON

I like to think these selfsame trees
Were budded in your springs the same,
And in these wood-walks where you came
You felt the selfsame westward breeze;

When autumn strips the oak trees bare
And, gaunt, the hornbeam twists the sky,
Remembering, poet, you and I
If not a time a place may share.

Impulsive, gypsy dark and strong,
You strode these paths amid the waste,
In agony of heart you paced
To bear the travail of your song,

Master, my unknown, unseen friend,
Whose thought with mine so nearly chimes,
What of the difference of our times?
You sought, I seek, the selfsame ends!

Your song that sings of weal and woe,
Your song that agonises still,
And loping down the little hill
Found the next way your verse should go.

(Tennyson lived at High Beech where he composed much of his elegiac poem IN MEMORIAM.)

FREDERIC VANSON

* Clare's Visitor

Sir, I do not know you.
My name is John Clare, and I am mad.
I have been kept here fifteen years.

Sir, you use words like
'paranoia' and 'schizophrenia':
perhaps you are an Italian.
We do not understand them here.
Sir, why do you labour so long
in the graveyard of my past?
I can no longer trap those songs of nature —
in my head now the mincing
curse of parakeets.

That gold I scratched for with my quill
is now a coin of memory debased.
Once my poems chuckled like water
over the quartz pebbles of their learning,
but fame was a greasy pole
that ill-served me as a perch.
Sir, they used me as a stitch
in their passing fashion of words,
then picked me out and replaced me
with some new-found brassy pin.
Sir, I must go now — I am tired.
Thank you for the Wordsworth poems;
I shall not read them.

* (John Clare was for a time a patient in an asylum near Epping, the setting for this poem).

STANLEY J. THOMAS

(Previously published in NEW POETRY and in A FADING OF GOLD [Poetry Essex].)

Sir Nicolas Conyngham Tindal
Chelmsford
1776-1846

He sits there
Eternally still
Carved in solemnity
Judging no-one now
An object of daubs
Slogans
And sparrows
That whiten his wig with innocence

A good man the inscription tells

So there he sits
In a sea of fumes and pommelling sound
Occassionally they come and scrub him down
Those fearless men from the Council
Whose forbears he judged
With wisdom
Kindness
And justice

Or so the inscription tells

JOHN JONES

14

In a Colchester Gallery

(portrait of an unknown girl)

She hangs like a footnote in space
worth more than a rationed side-glance
she blinks to room's white eye.

An arc-widening blur of pictures
full circles back to her,
she impinges uncannily.

Lean and upright sits the
girl (called maiden then),
her face a gown

of billowy smiles —
nutmeg-stuffed cheeks at sittings
belie the captured gaiety —

laughs down the centuries.
At what ? Her anonymity ?
I smile back at mine.

STANLEY J. THOMAS

The Old Woman of Latchingdon

She was old
Very old
And the tide of time
Had cast upon her rooms
A history of Queens and Kings
Written on penny things
Of china and tin
Sons in sepia
Incredibly young
A husband
Young enough to be her son
And that was how she lived
With double clocks in every room
And she knew
The thin comfort of their ticks

When they found her
Folded in the soft palm of quiet
They whispered
Because there was a dignity everywhere
And a hush of dust
That reminded them of some ancient tomb
Quaint with treasure
They saw in every room her double clocks
Stopped as she had been stopped
But then
She was old
Very
   Very
      Old

JOHN JONES

*The Old Woman
of Latchingdon
lived close to this
Christ Church
junction
(Michael Seymour)*

*A lazy morning
in the Essex
countryside, near
Terling
(Dennis Mansell)*

Mother and children pose for this family portrait (Dennis Mansell)

*Itinerant swan on
the River Crouch
(Dennis Mansell)*

Creatures

Itinerant Swan From The River Colne

Parallel with Frinton sward he flew,
Above a hovering sky-lark's note
That vied with sea gulls plaintive cries
And murmuring, mumbling,
Tumbling stones
Left abandoned on the strand
By percolating foam.

Rose hues of the dying day
Darkening his silhouette
On Easterly course with out-stretched neck,
And flip, flop, flapping wings,
Seeking sanctuary in the salt marsh night
Over upturned faces, his shadow swept,
Earthing his ungainly flight.

GRACE GAFNEY

My First One
(billericay, 1972)

there are men would tell you
of their first woman
— or worse, even of their first car

i like to ponder
on my first . . . badger

at just three minutes past three
on a february friday morning,
as i was walking
. . . let's face it, i was stumbling,
though the evening had been worth the walk
and i was happy to stumble

and there he was,
his claws clicking on the tarmac,
running — straight at me

'goodness,' i thought, 'my first one
and he's going to run right between my legs'
. . . but no, he was almost under my feet
then (swish!) up the bank beside me

already just a memory
. . . of stripes, pointing at me
along a narrow nose
. . . of white, silvered in the wan street light,
a shuffling, scuttling silver of night
comes alive

so that as i coasted home,
every black-and-whiteness in the shadows
said 'badger'

TULLY POTTER

23

Peacocks visit an Essex Garden

Two tiara crested heads, newly come,
inquisitive by open window space —
have you ever looked in a peacock's face
caught by the Land of Punt, pirates and rum?
Moving by sun-warmed walls the fine pair thrum
a royal measure, brightening the place
with molten blues and greens, the female's lace
of pale brown feathers cools the colours' hum.

In the tea-time heat they chose their perches,
she the sun-drenched fence, and he the highest
point of vantage, terracotta roof ridge.
They left at dusk, following their searches
for peacock paradise; they did not rest
for long, then melted through a magic hedge.

BARBARA JOY O'BRIEN

Previously published in 'Essex Countryside'

Badger Burial, Burstead

old root grubber, worm gulper,
slung low to ground,
close to grubs and shades of shrubs,
down-under delver
with paws cruel and canny enough
to claw your way there
— nor would you be out of countenance
beside the wombat, the platypus

hangover of merlin's reign,
past master of the snort, the snuffle,
the long snore . . . great snoozer
through light of day and white of snow,
the book of incantations
has closed on you
— you who gridded these gritty fields
into a crossword
only you could crack

history is bunk . . . and you are evidence
that the man meant what he said;
his probing panzer corps
seeks out you and all the old patrols

lower than ever now,
dearer to roots and to the gulping worms,
you turn unblinking
toward a winter without a waking,
shifting down into those shades
which gave you to us

TULLY POTTER

At Tollesbury, Birdwatching

Tread warily, unless you meant
To listen to the mud's murky language
Of squelches under your wellingtons,
It will submerge the birds' homely calm.

Let's set the scene for hush and Zeiss binoculars,
And call the birds to act on the mudflats'
Beaten pewter stage.
Gulls and gannets glide in, forgetting
The North Sea's noise of waves exploding
On rocks like balloons too near needles.

GILLIAN FISHER

A Tawny Shear Moth Seen in Old Wintry Wood

Ballerina moth!
Butterfly in leotard!
Whirring whitenesses.

OLIVE BENTLEY

Previously published in 'Essex Countryside'

Forest Squirrel at High Beech

He cannot disguise his russet rustle
as he dives furiously for cover —
disturbing a squall of ticker-tape leaves.

Nervous eyes dart earth-wards.
Mine squint towards the sun
seeing his lean shape pressed against the beech.

Then he evaporates — vanishes away
and I below, hand-clapping, calling,
see a last shooting star, a flash of silver tail.

JUDITH M. DAVIDSON

This squirrel proves to be an ideal model in Epping Forest (Dennis Mansell)

*Two swans grace
a lake in Epping
Forest
(Dennis Mansell)*

Town and Village

A fine timbered building in the north of the county at Great Chesterford (Dennis Mansell

Young anglers in a Chelmsford park
(Dennis Mansell)

*Little Bardfield
Hall and the
Church
(Dennis Mansell*

Mulberry Green — a pretty corner of Old Harlow (Dennis Mansell)

A young artist leaves her mark on the Essex sands — until the next tide (Dennis Mansell)

High Summer in Frinton

Couched in a cliff-face hollow,
At the mid-day hush
When the town holds it's breath,
And silence is heard
Like the missing tick
Of a Universal clock,
Compelling my gaze
To abandon the page
Of a stone propped book.

Leisurely, out of the pearly haze,
Gliding in to my narrowed view
Blinkered by charlock
And burgeoning gorse,
A serene old lady
Of river and coast,
A gaff rigged Essex barge.

Archaic sails lowering
A russet back-cloth,
To power boats towing
Tenacious skiers
Flirting with poise
And red marker buoys,
Strung out like bobbing balloons.

Casting adrift a farewell salute
Unseen, by the lady floating by,
Wraith-like fading into the mist
Merging shimmering sea and sky.
All too soon
She was out of sight.
Out of my sun filled afternoon.

GRACE GAFNEY

37

West Ham, *circa* 1930

The blind, wide town that saw my birth
A place of girders cranes and docks
Was all I knew of spinning earth
Except for small and scrubby parks
From whose parched grass arose no larks
But dusty chattering sparrows chirped
And squabbled by abandoned locks
Hinting at truths as yet unguessed;
A place of girders cranes and docks
Within whose small and scrubby parks
I learned to know the spinning earth
But did not hear the soaring larks
Nor sounds of creatures yet unseen
But learned how dusty sparrows chirped
Survival by abandoned locks;
And here I learned to see and hold
Small hints of beauties yet unguessed
And ways of creatures yet unseen
In that blind town that saw my birth.

FREDERIC VANSON

(Previously published in 'Essex Countryside')

Near Theydon Mount, Essex

The misted porcelain of a morning sky,
This mild damp winter moves in me.
Like a dark sea the chopped earth glisteningly
Waits its inevitable new birth,
Each rigid furrow a ripple of hope.

A smoke-screen of dumb trees leading to clouds
Smudges the green-less hillside
And the long artistic vista that winter shrouds
In its dull mystique is marked by
Homes, farms and the winding runs of lanes:

Its mild topography would have suited Constable.
And half my mind inclines here,
All worry seems eminently escapable
By the unbreakable peace of a pool's surface
Where clouds, not time, pass over its face
And admit not the hopeless beauties of a world of men.

WILLIAM OXLEY

(Previously published in 'Forest Poets Anthology')

Southend on Sea

A peppermint town
wrapped in cellophane light.

Madame Zola,
scaly in silver floats
a filament of words.
She's an old crustacean
tough as a whelk;
her smile sinks
through to the bone.

Each child is king
in his realm
of sand,
with its paper-flags
and banquet of lollipops,
chips and candy-floss,
toffee and shrimps.

Air is seasoned with salt;
the sun lays
down a stratum of gold.

ISOBEL THRILLING

Night Comes for Southend

Mudflats
glisten like the skin of some
sea-beast emerging
from the tide;
quilted with scales of light
that swallow sky.

Sail-boats;
moths on charred water
dipped in scarlet.

Voices build ladders
of sound
stretching into dusk for
children to climb
reluctantly from the beach,
leaving a landscape
soon to be quenched by moonlight.

ISOBEL THRILLING

(Previously published in 'Essex Countryside')

The Horn Dance at Thaxted

You conjure an old world
out of the fastness of the forests
ritual dancers
stag-men
breathing your animal magic
all over us
at this deep midsummer
in the gathering darkness.

You send a shiver of superstition
to our safe knowledge
memories of ignorance
call up the daunting power of the unknown.
You weave through our present
persuasions of our past
draw dark drama into pools of modern spotlight
the old woman following

and all the time the fiddle plays

that faerie music

BARBARA JOY O'BRIEN

(Previously published in 'Essex Countryside')

42

An Essex Town in Winter

A landscape of patchy broken snow lies
Across the vision, pale sunlight waters ice

In stiff pockets of mud, fat-daubed skies
Fill the world, and the imminent white-fall is stayed

Momentarily by a forced cloud-parting of light —
As I stand in a sea of still cold air.

The iced-town lies below me: sudden bright
Roofs of houses, red roofs ranged along steel streets —

Their frozen gardens with frost-stripped trees
Like twigs of death in orchards of mist.

I see a silver train snake through the cutting
From Theydon Bois; hear a distant spluttering

Of a car; and as the scene embedded in winter
Tries movement, I hear water trickle somewhere.

WILLIAM OXLEY

(Previously published in 'The West Essex Gazette & Guardian')

Whelk Stall, Leigh

no selling of seashells on this shore
— they deal in what went inside;
the fright of seeing is free

the shock of matching mentally
just one whelk to its shell shape
— no mistaking the form,
in a tight spiral to the tail-tip,
yet hard to find in this damp twirl
the delicacy of the drawing-room ornament

think how you held it to your ear
and listened for distant sea mysteries
— imagine the whelk's moistness
at your ear . . . imagine
the life of the thing

even in death, cooked through and through,
it clings to whelkness:
its look of a fishy icecream,
the end curling confidently upward
and finding no comforting shell
— but still a whelk, wholly,
uniquely and cheekily itself

think . . . would you, stewed so cruelly
from the shelter of your shell,
keep your essential twist
or would you un-kink, into something less?

TULLY POTTER

A fascinating clutter of the sea at Leigh-on-Sea (Dennis Mansell)

A young observer looks out across the River Blackwater at Maldon (Dennis Mansell)

Timbered buildings at Castle Hedingham (Dennis Mansell)

*View across the
River Crouch
from the Lower
road,
Latchingdon
(Michael Seymour)*

Latchingdon Fields

A night or two ago
I walked out in the dark,
The mild air through.

I saw the harrow's eyes,
Two golden lamps,
Bumping across the field,
Already ploughed.

Oh infinite to me
The wonder of all this,
The beam of light, the soil,
Straight furrows and long toil,
The turning beam of gold
Sweeping the long night field
What hope and faith it told.

PEGGY WHITEHOUSE

Sweyn's Castle, Rayleigh

Your castle, Sweyn, is one of the imagination,
A monument to a nation's invaders
Almost erased from the town.

The stones of your keep were taken
To rebuild the church, farmers
Have grazed their cattle on your ground

And now the site of your fortress
Is shadowed by a mill, whose sails are empty
Skeletons, restored only for show.

This is a measure of progress —
The feudal wars, the farm, and now a fantasy
Of which life relics may lay below.

ADRIAN GREEN

(Previously published in 'Beachgame', Sol Publications)

Park in Romford

In the park today
everyone
played with balloons
of sunlight.

Roses spun
scarlet windmills;
from prams
the newly-minted babies
laughed

at the lake,
where the moon last night
had buried
her silver ball.

ISOBEL THRILLING

Haiku — Saffron Walden 1

Grandfather traded
at the Corn Exchange — now I
read the Library.

Saffron Walden 2

still mourn the burning
of the Rose and Crown Hotel
Walden the poorer.

BARBARA JOY O'BRIEN

Upminster Windmill

The smock mill stands like a stopped clock,
instinct with the timbre
of sleeping machines.
A Rip Van Winkle kind of place,
the raucous symphony of mill-stones
blocked in a silence
that grinds
our peace to powder.

We climb between thick beams,
breathing their indefinable incense
of stored sunlight,
we grow into the cortex of rooms,
embedded in wood.
The guide pours out his sack of words;
from the boat-shaped cap
we track
the flow of flour,
new grist for the mill.

ISOBEL THRILLING

(Previously published in 'Essex Countryside')

53

Hockley Woods

In Hockley Woods lie down
and think colours, all the colours
you have seen and have not seen

taste sweet bitterness that floods the sense
in Hockley Woods
a girl with squirrels in her eyes

flurry of branches in the quick distance
faces sharp for innocence
trapped in its own trap.

You are sunlight through the leaves,
soft shadows falling, windless
but murmuring in Hockley Woods

and there are creatures to see our loving
warm bodies having sense
but nothing to do with names.

ADRIAN GREEN

Trinity Street, Colchester, Essex
A January Afternoon 1968

The wing-flapping pigeon in the Roman street
And the mossy shadows of Holy Trinity;
The minutes eaten up by the sharp tongue
of the frozen silence; and weak
sunlight struggling on tombs.

Time gazes at the ancient pattern
And even now above the clouds
of other days,
Shadow and light and air,
And in a glimpse, signs of eternity;
And walking, and death, and
day awakening;
Dawn and sunset; All in the stillness
of a winter afternoon.

PETER SHERRY

Claypitts Farm House, Thaxted

Beside the pond
they planted cherryplum and pear
a hundred years ago
red apples, too,
which glowed vermilion in the grass
as they do now
and all the apple trees gleamed green . . . . .
but that is not my subject
I want to speak of Rome —
a touch of Rome lies buried in that clay
and sleeps the centuries away.

The farmer, ploughing, happened to unearth
one day decades ago
a Roman tile, a hypocaust,
the hypocaust showed signs of fire
and was a flue.
A villa could be there
mosaic floor and Roman treasures too
perhaps a kiln, as Radwinter has found,
close to the clay pits, a few feet underground.
Down there waits Roman time, preserved.

BARBARA JOY O'BRIEN

Westcliff 1953

That year we bought a house close to the shore.
Bay windows, bulging from their wooden frames,
A tiny belvedere of saffron glass
That filled the hall with warm, religious light,
And roses in the garden, such a joy
When Summer comes and, with the sun, the flowers.
I walked the dogs along the river shores
And watched the mist blot out the Kentish fields,
And turn the sea to sky, the sky to sea.
One night, the wind came up and pushed the tide
Into the town and through the flower beds
And carried smartly painted little boats
To smash them on our flinty garden walls
And tore their dainty sails to shreds of threads
Which vanished in the streaming, roaring dark.
Our roses stifled under banks of sand.
Thrown seaweed clung like veins to broken walls.
There, the path, a shattered, little prow
Proclaimed the Seanymph, drowned among the flowers.

K. HAYES

On Rayleigh Mount

'et in hoc manerio fecit Suenue suum castellum'
          — Domesday Survey of 1086
(and in this manor Sweyn has made his castle)

I stand on your hill, Sweyn, and imagine
your stretched out county forested
through Hanningfield and Baddow.

Here was the hunting land of kings,
and vineyards you imported
bore the fruit of comfort.

Your mound is no longer a fortress
watching over the flat land of Saxons,
we fight no war within your counties

though a clutter of houses now lays
siege to your once proud vantage,
your serfs have inherited the town

and, knowing nothing of history,
screaming tribes of cops and cowboys
attack the Martians in your park.

ADRIAN GREEN

(Previously published in 'Essex Countryside' and 'Beachgame', Sol publications)

At Leigh

The days were endless, when I was a child.
The sun stayed high, the darkness never fell,
And I would walk the sands down by the shore.
Eternal day, eternal sun as well.

My mind can catch the feeling, even now.
The clinging mud, that sucked amid the stones.
The river smell, I wish I could forget
That's part of me now, lodged within my bones.

So I've returned, to taste a little more,
A vintage brew, with childhood far behind.
To watch that clear, dear light, that clasped me round,
The centre of a child's world fills my mind.

But childhood mem'ries cannot soothe a mind,
That aches with years of sadness. Adult pain
And sense of loss has driven me to earth
To find you by the river, once again.

K. HAYES

Delayed Spring — Old Harlow 1979

(I.M. G.W. Bentley)

This is the spring you did not see —
April's hyacinths, aubretia, daffodils
In riverside gardens.
On river bank
The February celandine
And February's coltsfoot
(First to defy without leaves
The cold which helped to kill you)
Miniscule suns
Naked, fragile bodies of flowers,
Defenceless,
Dauntless blooms of February coltsfoot
Now in April
Amid the hyacinths
Declare a delayed triumph.
May you, father, know the comfort
Of a late spring
In another time scale
Parallel with ours
All sun and celandines.

OLIVE BENTLEY

Country Matters

East Anglian Deluge

England clowns its rump
like an aloof mandrill,
sits on and coolly forgets.
Nothing happens so cannot change.
To live here is to unwind
the clock out of tomorrow,
to asthmaticize the last wind,
watch with the Flying Dutchman
awaiting the final wave
that never breaks.

O this encirclement of water!
But the deluge must wait.
From the Essex saltings
to the tuliped fen
all is held in pawn to the sea,
patient as a bird-sniffing cat.
Such menacing precursors
these heavy skirts of rain
that drag their hemlines above.

And yet there is a wager afoot:
when the last Cornishman,
dying of tourists,
sinks greyly in his bed,
here it will be breakfast as usual.

STANLEY J. THOMAS

Autumnal

brown, green, brown, green
— the colours of the scene ease the eye;
autumn has not yet confounded them

a lone tractor is alien red,
an insect irritating to soil and to serenity;
the farmer, known even from this far,
bows ageing at the wheel,
weathered face over green coat, brown trousers;
in the furled earth
a grounded cloud of gulls flounders

the eye, sweeping up and over the blind sky,
finds further furrows;
a plane traverses, pulling out its white plumes
to halve the blue pool

no figure there, familiar to the view,
the plane a mere badge against a uniform coat,
the man careering in it
immaterial to the issues of autumn;
a silver ghost of movement, ploughing grooves
which already some drunk ariel is erasing

down here the field is rich with brown cleavage
— it is here the birds hanker,
not after the ploughboy of the sky

the eye too will tire
of all that blatant blue,
those vivid cloud veils and vapour trails;
the shades of brown and green and in between
salve the autumnal soul

TULLY POTTER

Under Essex Skies

I drag legs of iron over
this swimming ploughland where
water has clamped its heavy gauge.
Paths and furrows an amorphous whole,
moulded soft under the hammer
of these dense Essex skies.
I am nailed in a frame between land and sea
yet seemingly beyond either.
No anchorage here for my land sail
in this primeval cataclysm.
There is above all the waste —
soil rushing liquid through gullies,
overbrimming the tangled ditches,
coating the roads like rusty rooftops,
pebbled, in contast, by carmine berries

from hedgerows smashed to shapelessness
by the screaming cross-wind.
Bales of rotting paper by the copse
are now sheep overcrowding in blank despair.
And down by Cobbins Brook a lone tree
has grafted a stilled bull to its bark,
otherwise I drown alone on this inland shore.
An ancestral echo of survival
gushes through the dammed tributaries of the mind
as this jam roll of weather unwinds
its relentless stodge, and, unlike Noah,
I am made uncomfortably aware
of the lack of cedar wood.

STANLEY J. THOMAS

*Angry clouds
threaten Maldon
(Dennis Mansell)*

A thatcher at work (Dennis Mansell)

Rowing boats waiting to be useful on a lake in Hatfield Forest (Dennis Mansell)

Daffodils herald
a new springtime
in a garden near
Thaxted
(Dennis Mansell)

Daffodils

shrill trumpets, elegant as telephones
and poised
to broadcast or receive;
random guardlights
gangling
over spiky pallisades

unpaid informers, lissom listeners
— the merest breath
setting them sniding

ageing gossips
wrinkling
into bitter, still-blonde harridans

mocking even death,
the lying-in-state
becoming a lying-in;
every last one
assured
of a two-faced renaissance

TULLY POTTER

The Pools

Some change, they say, some fall in the water table
Has left them like this, mere hollows
Now with a dribble of brackish stuff only,
Now sans fish, sans reeds, sans waterfowl.

But it was not so once. My childhood wondered
At the waterbirds and the roach quick in
                                    the clearness,
Stood amazed at the swan's width of wing
                                    and marked
The wake of the descending mallard
                        making great vees
Under willow and aspen.

It was not so once. Here the Sunday anglers,
Patient or obstinate, waited for a silvery catch
To spin at the line's end, gleaming in sunshafts.
Here in calm, remembered, anticyclonic days
The great trees nodded to themselves, perfectly
                                            imaged,
And all the park rang birdsung until Venus.

And all about were the great fields of childhood
In which the park gate was a good league distant
That's now a furlong; where grew to my
                                    astounded seeing
Harebells, primroses, unnameable tiny flowers
Like captive Plieades in a greensward heaven.

Some change, they say. And there's a change
                                    not least

In the beholder,
Himself diminished though Mays sing birdbright still.

FREDERIC VANSON

70

Forest

Unlike my Tapio-haunted, tongue-daunting
pinecushion on the wildmoor,
fir against waste wind,
this English forest drove me to words.

It was mildest December
when I walked its wide, contrasting spaces,
ducked cantilever branches,
scuffed copper-alloy mould
from beeches pillaring the clouds
with castellated chalice of trunks,
large old elm, larch,
arthritic oaks
and pines longing for the light.

And I was aware, too,
among these aged trees, of how
beneath the crackling cover,
deep-rotting roots of ancestors
burrowed to the bedrock,
an archaeology of vegetation,
and saw how ancient primitives
heard spirits whisper here,
saw goblins in the convoluted bark,
smelt monsters in the dwarf-stump outcrops,
and feared the witchwood.

So I faced again my own preoccupation,
felt the past presént itself to me,
tying me numb and dumb and wordless
in among the woods and weeds
and leaves leaving largesse for next year's growth,
knowing I must escape that I might make
my poem, for, with silence and with savage age,
this forest swamped the song
it made me sing.

(from 'All the Slain Soldiers')

MIKE SHIELDS

A Sonata of Summer

(Epping)

The yellowing path snaking and sloping
Past the field's fringe —
The silent sucking of July heat bringing
Butterflies gliding through airy sweat.

Sitting under such blue and gold
With this world crowned by a crown of song
Happiness seems altogether possible and old
Sun-sent like the Danaen shower,
But welling as well from within, a labidinal power
Of the simple and sensuous will
Through which we see this world
As seductive and bright and well lit
As the imprisoned goddess's womb became.

The yellow path burns at the field's fringe
The wild flowers colourfully nod
Bird songs crack in the scented heat
And butterflies crazily glide in the airy sweat.

WILLIAM OXLEY

Previously published in 'Poetry Newsletter' (Philadelphia)

The Road to Clavering

Brunettes in crinolines, the blossom boughs
are soft-lipped brides that sway the May-day in
here, in this quiet lane damp with the shade
out on the road to Clavering.
Decked in bright shirts, the young farm labourers
come riding on the hay wisped by the breeze
down narrow highways, chariot-wheeled
through this triumphal arch of trees.

JUDITH M. DAVIDSON

Looking at a Hill

On that wild hill
I see the robin-colour fade
Each tree with hollow mist
Its bark in-laid:

Each standing thorn,
With berries laden:
Each running brook,
The bracken, fading

To some dull brown: or leaf,
to russet turning:
And on the sumach tree
The red leaves burning

As Autumn fires,
And ancient byres,
Lit by old barns
Flicker at night away;
. . . I see my life
*   Returning.*

PEGGY WHITEHOUSE

The Aspens

Whispering together, summer on summer, these aspens
Have seen much come and go
In the eighty years or so
Since they first lifted from the Essex soil
Their tossing leaf-talk.
Once they were young amid rough fields
By a rough farmhouse, set in mud and droppings,
Reached by a rutted track, an old gate leaning
Like a village drunk on its sagging hinges. The cattle
Scratched their hides on their boles, the odour
Of pigs in muck moved about them in the July airs.

Only later came the Sisters, when these aspens
Had gossiped and sibillated for a generation
                              of men or more,
And the house grew, the rutted yard
Became a drive. About them a garden
Took shape under the spades of the brides of Christ,
And roses bloomed and bees visited and
                              lawn-searching birds.

Whispering together summer on summer the aspens
Remember time and change in this corner
                              of Essex quiet,
Content as the Sisters in their lot are,
Whispering together in service and prayer.

FREDERIC VANSON

from 'Hemingford Grey and other Poems' (Poetry Essex)

75

Morris Music

When Morris men come dancing through the town
with ribbons flying, then the music calls
to all who hear and summer song enthrals
as boots and bells chase rhythm up and down.

The pipe and fiddle charm the air, the brown
notes liquefy, the coloured music falls
in vivid bursts, and straight from greenland halls
young Pan appears decked in a flowered crown.

These dances are performed by Persian tribes
on isolated plains, stick with stick vies
and waving handkerchiefs resemble foam.

This music warms the heart and soul, it bribes
the senses to remember racial ties
and common origins: it takes you home.

BARBARA JOY O'BRIEN

(Previously published in 'Orbis')

Morris Men participating in the annual Morris Dancing Festival at Thaxted (Dennis Mansell)

The Essex Show is held each June at the Great Leighs showground (Dennis Mansell)

A sailmaker's loft
at Leigh-on-Sea
(Dennis Mansell)

A shaft of sunlight highlights a bough in an Essex forest (Dennis Mansell)

Forest Sequence
V

I see a city in this forest
Its shadowed highways threading leaves
Its wooden towers strong among the clouds,
A squirrel-built and bird-peopled city
With high dens and nests and stores of food
And little markets daily thronged
And places ringing with voices
I can never understand.

I see a city in this forest, a city
Of suspended parks on tufted branches
Of bridges crazy-perfect
And high holes with staggering views
Where squirrels have their ranches;
Whilst at night the watching owls patrol
The endless windy streets
Vigilant as gods in their eternal wisdom.

I see a city in this forest
A city built in leafy fields
At the verge of swaying sky
Beneath the browsing sun — a city
Just as complex as any built below
Yet less in violent conflict, this I know.

WILLIAM OXLEY

The Mind is its Own Place . . .

From my bed I see
Only the apple-tree:
Thin boughs showing
Black, against a dark sky —
But in my mind's eye
There is Debden Water flowing
And, cool beneath the beeches shade,
I see the green moss of Fulfen Slade;
And nothing can stop me going
To the secret places of my mind.

Mile by mile,
Through the field-gate, over the stile,
By the keeper's track to the high wood winding;
Skirting the ruined barn (more frightening now
In my dream walk through the apple-bough)
Where a bramble-curved milestone hides,
                        still sending
Travellers 'TO DEBDEN and CAMBRIDGE'
                        — just as though

Anyone now would go
(Through this wilderness of no ending)
To either place from here!

. . . .

I am tired from my mind's roaming
And I enjoy, even a-bed, the home-coming
To the window-square and the dark apple-boughs
And the day's breaking and the nights close.

PHYLLIS HARRISON

Memorial to an Essex Hedge

At dawn the Traveller saw
The vibrant hedge; green it was,
Alive with insect rustling and birdsong,
Twining tendrils, thorns, blossoms and
Deep secret places
Safe in the year's springtime.

At evening the Traveller passed
The same hedge; sad it was
Hacked and broken, cringing at the sky
Blackberries and dog roses never
To know the sun's kiss
Slashed in the year's springtime.

In between, the Traveller knew,
Came the blade; loud it was
Devouring all before it, beauty and
Good husbandry distained.
And now a small bird searched forlorn,
Mute in the year's springtime.

Long ago the Traveller met
Old Ted the hedger; proud he was
Sharpening his knife, trimming and weaving.
The nest empty, the bounty gathered in
He had waited for
The year's dying time.

MARGARET SPARKS

83

Winter in High Essex

Over the groundbass of these upturned fields
Hard-cloven and heavy with the yield of years,
The clouds make a continual counterpoint,
Now like visible madrigals, now sweet airs,
Or piling up in majestic passacaglias.
On certain days the mist creates a backdrop
Of islanded trees, elm groups and lonely oaks,
The berried hedgerows constellate a deep green
And rooted heaven. The curve of the fields
Is older than Essex kingdom, only bared
By the axe and the fire of the Saxon, but retaining
The same whalebacked rise and fall. The winds
Whistle shrill pipings through bush and briars
While over the groundbass of these upturned fields
The clouds make a continual counterpoint.

FREDERIC VANSON

Previously published in 'Inscape' (Canada)

The snow trail of a lone winter traveller near Kelvedon (Dennis Mansell)

*The sun glistens
on this snowy
Essex scene
(Dennis Mansell)*

*Stebbing from the air
(Dennis Mansell)*

Looking towards Harlow new town on a bright winter's day (Dennis Mansell)

Thousands of tourists visit Finchingfield in the summer, but during a winter snowstorm local children have the village to themselves. (Dennis Mansell)

*Blossom time at
Silver End, near
Witham
(Dennis Mansell)*

Thatched cottages at Stebbing Green (Dennis Mansell)

*Low tide on the
River Blackwater
at Maldon, a
favourite haunt
for daytrippers
during the
summer.
(Dennis Mansell)*

Written in a Field
Near Maldon

Let me die
Now
In a shroud
Spun gold
From the old October sun
Die
Now
Among the red-run leaves
With England
Ploughed and brown
It seems
A good time to die now
As birds
Journey down the sky
In slow dark streams
And webs cry
Their first grey dew

In a shroud
Spun gold
From the old October sun
Among the red-run leaves
To a lonely robin's song
Let me die
Now

JOHN JONES

Bell Common, Epping

The wet sentiment of grey-green grass
On the morning upland of this tufted common;
The sprawling brambles in their summer mass
Sharply-fruited and sweet as a woman's lips;
Above all the forest's tall verge hovering nearby
With its drifting smell sustaining the air:
An especial love, a joy is always there
For one who wanders openly, free among
The small grief of bended leaf
With the birds' indecipherable song
And the intelligible ripple of sky above.

WILLIAM OXLEY

(Previously published in 'Littack')

Sea, River and Estuary

Trawling For Sprats Off the Essex Coast

I saw
Greyness,
Thrown over the day.
A bow-string of
Horizon,
Taut
Across the arc
Of sea and sky.

I saw
Grey gulls.
Hovering hopefully
In the wake of
Trawlers
Chug, chugging,
Hugging the shore
Like splashing matrons,
Dragging behind them
Skirts
That billowed,
Flashing with
Thrashing silver,
Stirring the calm,
The stillness that was grey.

GRACE GAFNEY

(Previously published in 'Essex Countryside')

The weak sun fights a losing battle with storm clouds at Leigh-on-Sea (Dennis Mansell)

By the River Crouch

"Those who trespass will be prosecuted!"
You can read the sign.
Why, therefore, do you march past regardless
Opening the white gate wide
And commanding me with your eyes.
I have no choice but to follow.
We wheel our bikes through the fields
Pass cows grazing unremarked
My discomfort subsiding;
You are always different
In choosing you, I chose a new world.
A different law.
In opening the gate, we enter upon a mystery.
Never before has the grass been so lush and green
The trees so still and holy.

We run delighted between the corn
Fall tumbling amidst the reeds.
Leaving our bikes beneath the trees we run
Run until the wind whistles through us
And whisks us up in one great torrent of power
Depositing us in ecstasy on the river bank.
Naked we plunge into the gleaming water
Swim like fish through the shallows
The sun turning your skin to silver
Beautiful to behold.
Lazily I lean against your warm strength
Enter with joy this second Eden.
Why must a harsh voice break into this sanctuary
Shattering the still-ness?
The woman on the bank is hysterical.

This is Her land, Her beach,
Her cows who will break their hooves on the bikes
— We will find *them* at the police station.
Who are we anyway, as we tumble into our clothes,
And spring to face this vision on the bank?
Why are you so calm, whilst fear causes me to tremble,
And to pour forth words of expiation.
Why fear?   The vision is not so terrible —
Having need of contact, she yet has banished all.
In the gently sympathy flowing and encompassing her
She blossoms and gives forth scent.
We cross the fields together, talking.
Her daughter has come down to meet us.
Laughing, we collect our bikes, not at the police station,
And enter the private realm of the inner sanctuary

Here, marrows are broken for us
Tomatoes gathered, tempers soothed.
The monster has become an angel of light
Dispensing sweetness.
We enter into her loneliness
Partake of her sorrows.
Bitter the grapes of the unbeloved
Picked with unloving hands.
Sweet, those which ripen in a new made sun.
"Come to our cottage tonight
We have little, but offer you our all."
The daughter, overwhelmed, stoops from her rich prison
To enter the little world we have created.
That night, in long silk skirt and sequins
She shares bread at the board of a King.

CLARE KENDALL

Early visitors have the beach to themselves as the summer sun tries to break through the early morning mist, at Leigh-on-Sea. (Dennis Mansell)

June by the Estuary

Early summer or late spring?
it is a matter of names only,
this is the loveliest of seasons.
By the slow estuary, under a huge sky,
hear the perpetual hush hush of the rushes,
contemplate the aerial ballet of the tender grassheads
a foot above the eye, and mark against the sky
the eight-foot sentinel grasses.

The sun is warm as maidslove;
feel the wind's kindness, sense
the blessing of seacoming air
with its hint of the three-mile tides
tangy and salt amid the greenness
of this other and different England.

The river, inch by slow inch
raises its tides,
over the moss-green silt and the scattered stones,
the shelduck, level in flight,
honk up the reach and down.

See here in this loveliest season
the hundred shades of green
the subtleties of yellow, the rarer reds,
learn how the blue sky alters
from zenith to level distances far as Cathay.

It is a rich land, top-heavy with yield and fruitful,
Of scattered copses, single sentinel trees,
and a land of sweet musics,
the hush hush of the rushes, the whispering sedges,
and over the small butterflies, acrobatic by grassheads,
the sound of skylarks fills the all-day sky.
This, under a huge flawless heaven
by the slow tides of the estuary
is the loveliest of seasons,
under the light winds' kindness,
under the love of the lifting and lyric sun.

FREDERIC VANSON

Droughtbreak — Mersea Island

There was little joy in the ride: exhausted
fields scorched and the new-ploughed earth like granite;
cows in this lion-land pining for meadow pasture.

And death croaked by the road: the gaunt
hedges bearing an unwept agony
of small lives, gesturing stark defeat.

Afternoon cumulus piled again: mocking
promise without credit,   only the gathered
sweat of a hot land.   Rain was a lost bounty.

Then there was water before us: the salt
estuary tide engulfing the road — a rippled
bitter sea-flow swilling the rancid asphalt . . .

as shadowed clouds descended over the mirrored
reeds,   and rags of rain-cloud brushed the swollen
marsh,   the aching brown of the hazy island.

And so came the relenting: showers falling
fast on shimmering sheets in rising silver,
far columns of water-light,   and limpid

pale distance dissolving in gentle reflection.
Downpour blessing.   I shall be glad for ever
to have met the grey water and the rain together.

MARGARET TOMS

Stort in a Calm October

Many, many are the mirrors
That men for trade or for art
Have silvered, ovalled, bevelled and framed.
The ancients also loved them, polishing metal
To show themselves their faces
Or better, to double the beloved's image.
But here art and craft model upon nature.
Narcissus needed no bronze, no speculum metal,
To fall into that fatal and fell self-love.
Nor today do clouds, trees, hovering birds,
Need any glass but the river's glass
So still it is in anticyclonic October,
So unbroken by even a rumour of wind.

Look! the world's upside down and every
Angle of bank, bifurcation of branch,
Every twig's, every grassblade's image
Is perfect, unaltered, antiphonal.
Cloud answers cloud, birds are two birds
Arcing two skies, and all things
That up-reach, spread, soar, overarch,
Can love, like Narcissus
Their own innocent and watery image!

FREDERIC VANSON

Foundations (Stort Navigation)

Just back from the navigation's edge discover
The ground plan of the place, a grid in bricks,
Rufous and crumbling between grass and nettles.
Here must have been the kitchen, see how tiles
Still sketchily suggest domestic order
Though most are gone. And here the front room watched
The plodding horse, the hayload on the barge,
The bargeman's boy leading them Londonwards.
And see over here where still the tiny garden's
Stubborn survivors challenge the docks, the tangles.
Here careful wives hung out proud snow white sheets,
The breeches and skirts of children, petticoats
By tens no doubt, or dozens.

Two centuries since, or the best part of two,
Children woke to the world here, eyes learning
The fleck of reflected ripples on the ceiling,
Ears learning to interpret the plod-plod of horses,
The cry of plovers, the lip-lap of water,
The songs and calls of the bargemen, the groan
Of the too-frequent locks a stone's throw away.
Two centuries or so since when this ageing water
Was fresh as April and the latest wonder
Someone and someone's wife and someone's children
Loved, hated, hoped, despaired, married
                                                  and gave in marriage,
While the bright waters and the brighter barges
Slid slowly, slowly to the heard-of city
By tens no doubt, or dozens.

FREDERIC VANSON

Sailing Barges off Southend

Drifting on a tide from long ago,
They swing at anchor silently
Wreathed in early morning mist,
Like ghosts grown mellow with antiquity.

With names like Gladys, Will and Edith May
Heroic legends motionless on ancient bows,
They are waiting for the breeze, patiently
Submissive to the whims of air and ebb.

Later with windlass rattling as anchors are raised
Sails set at the stirring of wind over tide
They bear away a pageant of remembered trade,
A flock of stately seabirds through the lanes.

ADRIAN GREEN

Estuary

The country's wrong for coral,
Wrong for coral necklaces, for ivory carving,
Incense.
Here is mud: light glowing grey:
Sail-barges billowing on the flat water.
Several horizons: the sea wall: the sky:
And the creeks
Which betray:
Which at low tide are paddling pools:
Which at mid-tide challenge the adventurous:
Which at high tide strand and drown.
His name was Colin, he was seven or eight,
He stuck in the mud and drowned, from the water.
Sunk into the mud,
Into the worm-casts and crab-shells,
The pearl disintegrated,
The illuminated sea-mist of the estuary
Covered the memory of the pearl.
The fishermen are yoked with cockles,
They bring home the cockles,
Bring home the harvest,
Home the corn of the fields of the sea,
Home to us here, waiting on the quayside.

JOHN ABRAHAMS

Sea-sculpture at Frinton

A glass chunk, sea-smooth,
hollows the beach.
Its rich, green shape fits cool
into the hand;
fingers follow the curves
of imprinted waves.
Here star rims cut their silver,
fish have left self-portraits.
Here lie impacted storms,
thin bones of light.
Hold with care the unlit caves
of wrecked voices,
where the wind lies curled
among dull gold of drowned coins.
Look at the sky
through this stone inlaid with sunsets;
feel the psychometry
of the sea.

ISOBEL THRILLING

(Previously published in 'Essex Countryside')

Daybreak Over the Mudflats

Flame streaked clouds pursue the rim of night,
Dappling gold the misty creeks below,
A creeping tide uprights the dinghies' masts
And caresses the oystercatcher's toes
As they bow their heads to the morning rites,
   And lapwings dance on the wildfowler's hide.

Beyond the headland,
The curlew's cry on the rising wind
That parts the quivering reeds
And ruffles the shelduck's back,
   Breaks the estuary calm.

GRACE GAFNEY

(Previously published in 'Essex Countryside')

Two youngsters survey a deserted Clacton beach (Dennis Mansell)

Memories are made of this. Fishing during the summer vacation in the River Blackwate at Coggeshall. (Dennis Mansel

*Riverside
cottages at
Colchester
(Dennis Mansell)*

Braxted Park, on a Sunday afternoon when it is occasionally open in aid of charities (Dennis Mansell)